The
Wonderland of
PLANTS

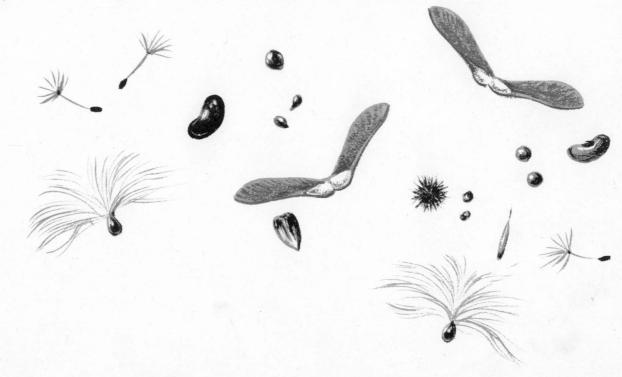

THE WONDERLAND OF PLANTS

BY

TERRY SHANNON

ILLUSTRATED BY

CHARLES PAYZANT

ALBERT WHITMAN & COMPANY · CHICAGO

DEDICATION

It is with gratitude that we acknowledge the kindness of Mildred E. Mathias, Ph.D., Associate Professor of Botany at the University of California at Los Angeles, in checking the manuscript and art work for this book.

Terry Shannon and Charles Payzant

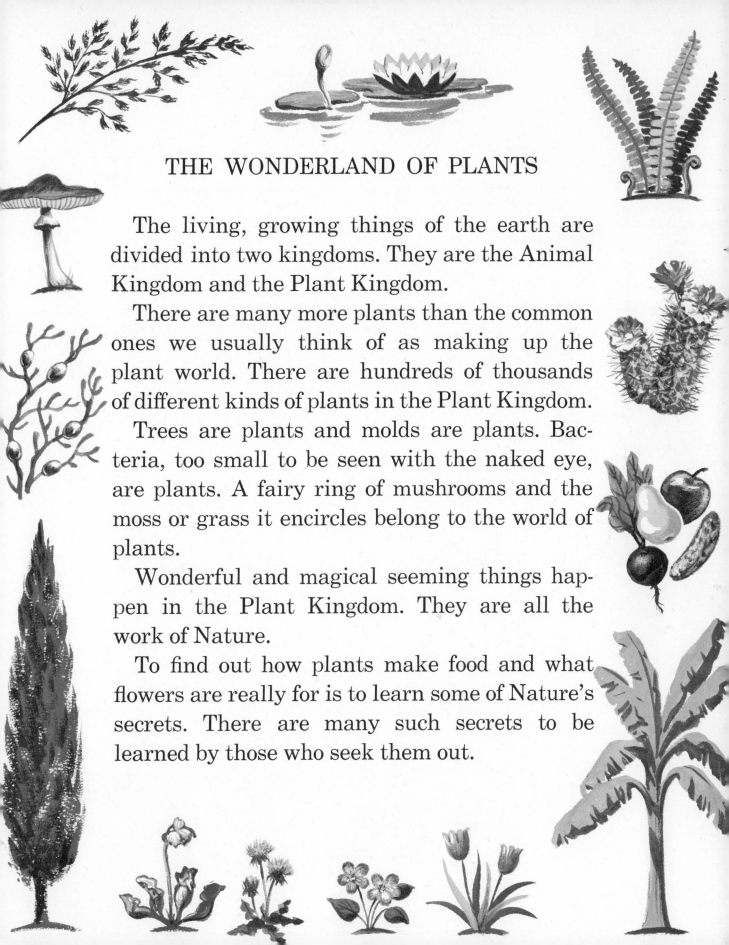

THE WONDERLAND OF PLANTS

The living, growing things of the earth are divided into two kingdoms. They are the Animal Kingdom and the Plant Kingdom.

There are many more plants than the common ones we usually think of as making up the plant world. There are hundreds of thousands of different kinds of plants in the Plant Kingdom.

Trees are plants and molds are plants. Bacteria, too small to be seen with the naked eye, are plants. A fairy ring of mushrooms and the moss or grass it encircles belong to the world of plants.

Wonderful and magical seeming things happen in the Plant Kingdom. They are all the work of Nature.

To find out how plants make food and what flowers are really for is to learn some of Nature's secrets. There are many such secrets to be learned by those who seek them out.

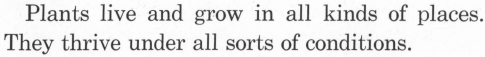

T A S T E S
D I F F E R

Plants live and grow in all kinds of places. They thrive under all sorts of conditions.

They grow in mountain snows and they grow in the water. They grow in the blazing heat of the desert and in the gloomy dampness of rain belts. Flowers push through the ice to bloom in arctic cold. Mosses and lichens grow at the other tip of the world in the antarctic.

Some plants like it hot, some cold; some like it dry and some damp since tastes in growing conditions vary.

But there is some form of plant life almost everywhere, except in the total blackness of the deep sea where no sunlight ever penetrates.

1 ALGAE

FUNGI

PLANTS ARE DIVIDED INTO FOUR GROUPS

There are many ways of classifying plants. One way is to put them into four big groups: Algae, Fungi, Ferns, and Seed Bearing Plants.

All living things are made of the same basic matter. It is protoplasm, a jelly-like material. It is packed in tiny units called cells. Some plants have only one cell. Most plants have millions of them.

And most plants contain green coloring matter called chlorophyll. With chlorophyll they can make their own food from water, air and light. Plants that have chlorophyll are called green plants.

All but one of the four groups, fungi, are green plants. Each group has special things about it that make it different from the others.

If they have similar tastes, plants from each group may grow in the same area. They form plant communities.

3 FERNS

4 SEED BEARING PLANTS

ALGAE

Algae are the most simple of the green plants. Some grow on land but most grow in the water. More grow in salt water than in fresh water.

Green scum of ponds and lakes is algae. Seaweeds are algae. There are tiny algae of only one cell, while some of the seaweeds grow to be hundreds of feet long.

Many seaweeds cling to rocks or piling by growths called holdfasts. These are sometimes mistaken for roots. Algae have no real roots, stems or leaves. Plant bodies are made up of ribbons or masses of cell tissue. Material for making food is taken directly into the cells.

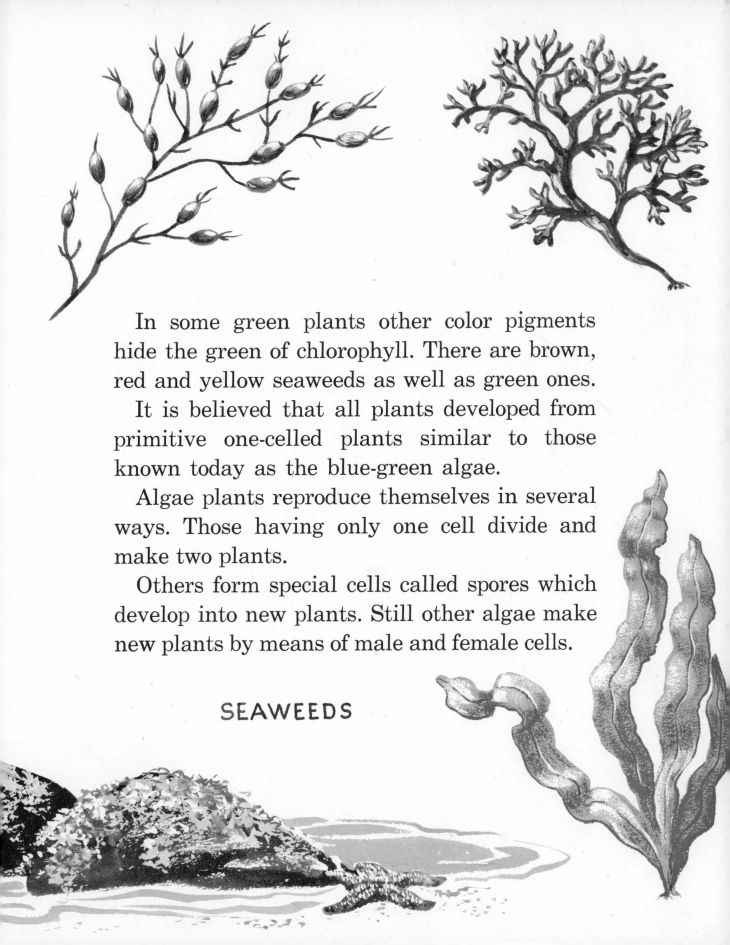

In some green plants other color pigments hide the green of chlorophyll. There are brown, red and yellow seaweeds as well as green ones.

It is believed that all plants developed from primitive one-celled plants similar to those known today as the blue-green algae.

Algae plants reproduce themselves in several ways. Those having only one cell divide and make two plants.

Others form special cells called spores which develop into new plants. Still other algae make new plants by means of male and female cells.

SEAWEEDS

PENICILLIN MOLD
(MAGNIFIED)

FUNGI

Fungi have no roots, stems or leaves. Since they have no chlorophyll they can't make their own food. They live on animals or other living plants or on dead plant and animal material.

Yeast from which bread is made is a fungus plant. So is the mold sometimes found on food. Penicillin is made from certain food molds.

Bacteria, too small to be seen without a microscope, are fungi. Some bacteria cause certain diseases. Others do helpful things. Some break down dead plants and animals so they can be taken back into the soil. This enriches the soil for growing things.

BACTERIA
(MAGNIFIED)

PUFFBALL

Mushrooms are fungi. Rusts and molds sometimes seen on trees and fruits are fungi. So are
the slimy molds seen in the woods. Some of these
things are beautiful when seen under a microscope.

Like algae, fungi plants reproduce in one of
three ways. Those of one cell split and make
two. Some fungi make spores which grow into
new plants. The powdery dark stuff that pours
from a dry puffball is millions of tiny spores.
These may drift on the wind for miles. Other
fungi reproduce by means of male and female
cells.

SHELF
FUNGUS

REINDEER MOSS –
A LICHEN

OLD MAN'S
BEARD –
A LICHEN

A third plant is formed by a fungus and an alga living close together as partners. Plants formed in this way are the lichens found on rocks and trees.

Bit by bit lichens break down rocks and help to form new soil. They are often mistaken for moss and several have the word moss in their names.

Mosses are green plants. But they don't fit neatly into one of the three groups of green plants. They are a bridge between plants that grow in the water and those that grow on land.

Mosses spread over wide areas in damp and shady places. A few grow under water. Slender threads hold the plants down and absorb water. Bits of growth are sometimes called stems and leaves. But they are not fully developed ones.

Mosses bear spores in cups on the end of little stalks. The spores grow into plants with male and female cells. These plants in turn bear spores.

MOSS
SPORE
CUPS

PINCUSHION
MOSS

A BRACKEN FIDDLEHEAD UNFURLS

FERNS

Ferns have real roots and stems and leaves. Their stems grow underground except for those of tree ferns.

One of the interesting things about most ferns is the way their leaves unfold. In the spring new leaves push up from the stem, curled up tight like the scroll of a fiddle. The fiddleheads slowly unfurl, opening out into graceful new leaves.

Fern reproduction, like the mosses, is in two steps. Spores grow in cases on fern leaves, usually on the back. When the cases snap, spores are flung into the air, then fall to the ground.

From these grow small plants, each with male and female cells. When these are joined by a drop of dew or rain, a new plant forms. It grows into the big plant on which spores grow.

POLYPODY FERN

FIDDLEHEADS

FERN SPORES

MAIDENHAIR FERN

SEED BEARING PLANTS

The most highly developed of all the plants are those that bear seeds. There are more plants in this group than in any other.

Here are familiar plants. Pine and oak, palm and apple trees. Buttercups and roses, violets and cattails. Water lilies and dandelions and bluebells. Corn and peanuts, wheat and lawn grass. Beets and lettuce, strawberries and water-melons. All these and many more bear seeds.

These plants have true roots, stems (a tree's trunk is its stem) and leaves. They have a flower of some kind even though we might not think of them as such.

Roots, stems, leaves and flowers perform special services. They work together to keep the plant alive and growing and to bear more of its kind.

LEAVES

VEIN
SYSTEMS

Leaves are usually thin and most are broad. But not all because narrow pine needles are leaves. Some leaves are made up of many small leaflets.

The flat part of a leaf is called the blade. This is stretched over a framework of ribs called veins. Some leaves have a heavy midrib. There are several types of vein systems. They are named for familiar things they look like.

PINNATE -
LIKE A
FEATHER

PARALLEL

PALMATE-
LIKE A
HAND

The leaf blade is attached to a leafstalk called a petiole. The petiole grows from the stem or a branching part of it.

Leafstalks twist and turn to place the blade where it will get the best light.

Most leaves turn their broadest part to the sun. But during the heat of the day in hot dry places some plants turn their leaves edgewise to the sun. This is to keep them from losing too much moisture.

Whatever their size, whatever their shape, leaves are where plants make their food.

OPPOSITE

ALTERNATE

WHORL

COMPOUND
LEAVES
MADE UP OF
LEAFLETS

PLANTS WORK HARD

Leaves take in air and send it out again through tiny cell openings called stomata. The plant takes carbon dioxide from the air and puts oxygen back into it.

Water is drawn from the earth into the plant by the roots. The water, bearing dissolved minerals from the earth, is taken up through the stem then into the leaves through their veins.

With chlorophyll present in the leaves, water and carbon dioxide combine to form sugar. This is done with energy drawn from the sun. Sugar is changed into starch and in some plants into oil and protein.

This liquid food is sent to all parts of the plant. Plants usually make more food than they need for daily use. They store the extra food in roots, stems, leaves, seeds and their containers.

An apple is a fleshy seed container. It takes the work of about forty leaves to make one apple. It takes only about ten leaves to build all the bananas on one stalk because the food making area of a banana leaf is so great.

FLOWER MAKES SEEDS
FOR FUTURE PLANTS

ACTION OF SUN ON
CHLOROPHYLL IN THE
LEAVES RESULTS IN
THE PRODUCTION
OF SUGAR FROM
CARBON DIOXIDE
AND WATER —
THIS PROCESS
IS CALLED
PHOTOSYNTHESIS

LEAVES RELEASE
OXYGEN INTO THE
AIR WE BREATHE

LEAVES ABSORB
CARBON DIOXIDE
FROM THE AIR

FOOD IS PUMPED
DOWN STEM FOR
STORAGE

ROOT SYSTEM
PUMPS MOISTURE
AND MINERAL
FOODS FROM THE
GROUND UP TO
THE LEAVES

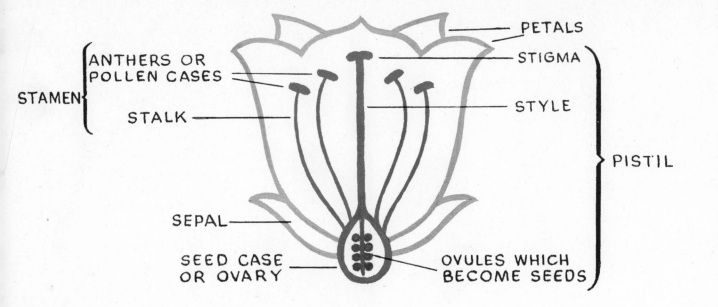

PETALS

STIGMA

STYLE

PISTIL

STAMEN

ANTHERS OR
POLLEN CASES

STALK

SEPAL

SEED CASE
OR OVARY

OVULES WHICH
BECOME SEEDS

FLOWERS

Flowers have special parts that work together to make seeds.

Just beneath the petals of a flower is a ring of leaflike parts called sepals. The sepals and petals protect the inner seed making parts.

Pistils are the female parts of flowers. At its base a pistil widens out. This area is called the ovary. Flower eggs, produced in the ovules, are in this protected place.

Stamens are the male parts of flowers. Pollen, usually a yellow dust, grows in a little case on the end of each stamen.

In some plants both male and female parts are in one flower. In others they are not.

Pollen and eggs must be joined before seeds can form. Most flowers cannot do this for themselves. The wind, water, birds and insects do it for them. They carry pollen from one flower to another.

Some plants such as the Easter Lily have simple flowers. Each blossom is just one flower. Others are not so simple. A sunflower blossom is made up of many tiny, tiny flowers within a ring of ray flowers. There may be as many as a thousand or more of the tiny flowers on one flower head.

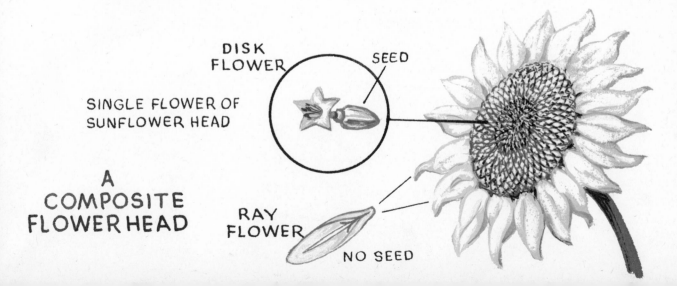

DISK FLOWER

SEED

SINGLE FLOWER OF SUNFLOWER HEAD

A COMPOSITE FLOWER HEAD

RAY FLOWER

NO SEED

We all enjoy the beauty of flowers. We enjoy their lovely colors, delicate perfumes and their many different shapes. And most of us have sipped the sweet nectar of honeysuckle or clover.

But Nature did not supply these delights just for our pleasure.

The bright colors of flowers, sweet smells and hidden nectar serve another purpose. They all play a part in the business of making seeds.

These are the things which attract birds and bees and other insects. Because of them plants are sure of helpers to carry pollen from flower to flower.

Flowers that depend on the wind or water to carry pollen have no need for gay colors, scent or nectar.

NECTAR LIES
DEEP WITHIN
FLOWER

BEE COMES
SEEKING NECTAR

POLLEN STICKS TO
BEE'S POLLEN BASKET

Bees are attracted to certain flowers because of their nectar. This is the material from which they make honey. Pollen is dusted onto the bee as it pushes into the flower to get the nectar. Pollen brushes off the bee onto the next flower it visits.

POLLEN
BASKET

Some flowers have their nectar deep within long blossoms. Hummingbirds reach into these with their long beaks. They service many flowers but are especially drawn to red ones. At the next stop they leave pollen on the pistil of another flower.

When a pollen grain from one kind of flower reaches a pistil of the same kind of flower it sends down a tiny tube into the ovary. Thus flower eggs are made ready to grow into seeds.

POLLEN IS BRUSHED OFF
ON PISTIL OF NEXT FLOWER

SEEDS

A seed is a baby plant wrapped up in a coat for protection. Within the seed are tiny roots, stem and leaves.

These parts are not yet able to make their own food. A supply of it is packed around the little plant inside its coat.

The seed lives on this stored food while it rests in the earth, then sprouts and starts to grow. In warm, moist earth it breaks out of its coat and pushes up into the sunshine.

The pressure of growing plants in reaching for sunlight is very great. Most everyone has seen a few thin blades of grass or other plants pushing up through cement to reach the light.

If conditions are right, the young plant that has pushed up through the soil develops into a mature plant. The mature plant in turn produces new seeds. Thus seed bearing plants continue to grow on the earth.

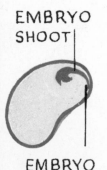

EMBRYO SHOOT

EMBRYO ROOT

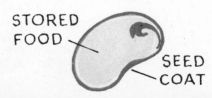

STORED FOOD

SEED COAT

BEAN SPLIT OPEN TO SHOW INSIDE

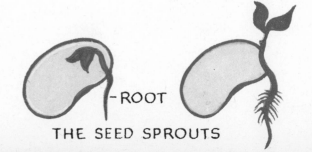

ROOT

THE SEED SPROUTS

1 THE SEED IS
PLANTED

2 IT SPROUTS
ROOTS AND
STEM

3 LEAVES
UNFOLD

4 BUDS ARE
FORMED

LET'S SEE WHAT HAPPENS WHEN WE PLANT A SEED

5 THE BLOSSOM
UNFOLDS

6 BLOSSOM IS
POLLINATED

7 SEEDS ARE FORMED
AS BLOSSOM
FADES

8 THE SEEDS FALL
- - - AND FIND
NEW LOCATIONS
WHERE THEY WILL
START THE CYCLE
OVER AGAIN

SEEDS IN CASES

Pine trees bear naked seeds that lie on the scales of the cone, protected only by the seed coat. But Nature has put an outer case or container over the coats of most seeds. There is a single seed in some. In others there are many.

Pods, berries, fleshy fruits, corn husks and coconut husks are seed containers. They protect the seeds while they are forming. And they protect them when they leave the parent plant to seek a growing place.

If all seeds dropped beneath the parent plant they wouldn't have enough room to grow. Wind, water, animals and people carry seeds away from the parent.

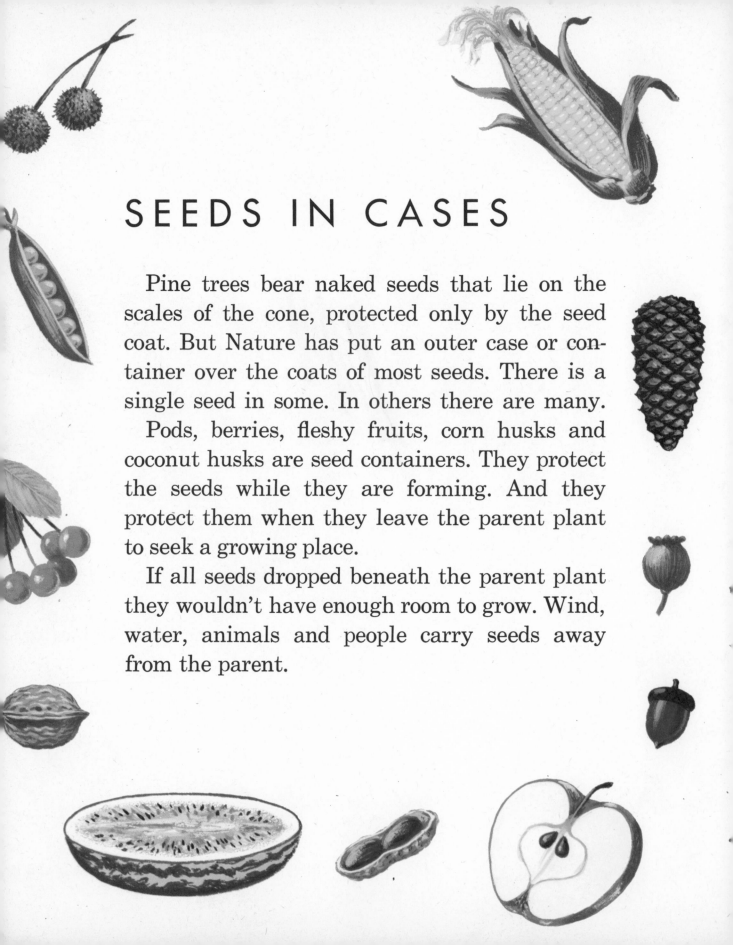

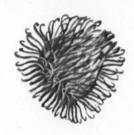

BURDOCK

TUMBLEWEED

HITCH HIKERS, FLYERS AND POPPERS

VIOLET

Some seeds hitch a ride with animals or people. They catch hold of fur or clothing by tiny hooks or sticky material.

Some seeds are eaten by birds and animals and carried away. Seeds may fall, unharmed, in droppings and grow far from the parent plant.

Little parachutes carry dandelions and similar seeds through the air. Seeds like the maple whirl along on tiny blades.

MILKWEED SEEDS

Wild geranium seeds are flung into the air when the seed case snaps. The seeds pop out with such force they land some distance away. Violet seeds are squeezed out by the twisting of the dry pod.

WILD GERANIUM

MAPLE

DANDELION

COCKLEBURR

CAT-TAIL

SOME PLANTS DON'T NEED SEEDS

A bulb is a package of stems and leaves with a bud in the center. The leaves are full of stored food. Underground, they divide and make more bulbs from which new plants grow.

Onions and lilies are plants that reproduce in this way as well as bearing seeds.

Some plants, such as crocuses and gladioli, grow from corms which look something like bulbs but are solid. Food is stored in an inner stem.

A potato is an underground stem which has stored up a large amount of food. The eyes of a potato are really buds.

When the buds sprout, a young plant is in the making. It lives on the stored up food, sends roots down into the soil and leaves above ground. It soon becomes a new plant able to make its own food, flower and bear seeds.

BULBS

POTATO

EYES

RUNNERS

CUTTINGS

Other seed bearing plants too have other ways of making new plants. Some send out runners which take root wherever their leaf and bud parts touch the ground. Some plants send out little shoots. Still others sprout from a leaf.

Some plants, such as geraniums, will put out roots from a cutting placed in the earth or in a pot.

LEAF SPROUTS

SHOOTS

DANGER, BEWARE

Many plants attract us by their beauty but may spell danger if we aren't careful in handling them.

There are many plants that spell danger to insects too. Some attract insects then trap them and use them as extra food. Plants of this kind are called meat eaters or carnivorous plants.

Leaves of the Venus fly trap snap shut when insects land on them. The edges lock the leaf together while juices digest the prisoner.

The pitcherplant has leaves at its base that become partly filled with water. Insects going to them to get a drink sometimes slip and fall in. Hairs which point to the bottom of the cup keep the insects from getting out so they drown. The plant draws food from the insect as it decays.

PITCHER
PLANT
LEAF

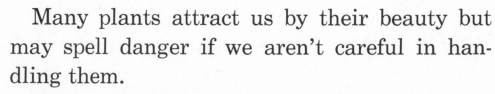

POISON IVY

POISON
OAK

VENUS FLYTRAP
LEAF SNAPS SHUT

SUNDEW LEAVES
HAVE STICKY HAIRS

WHAT PLANTS MEAN TO US

Without the Plant Kingdom there could be no Animal Kingdom. There would be no people, no animals.

Everything we eat and everything that animals eat can be traced back to plants. If there were no green leaves making food, there would be no life at all.

Even the animals that eat only other animals could not live without plants. Because the animals upon which they feed eat plants or still other animals that do.

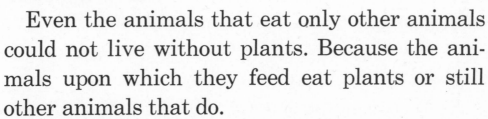

Plants provide us with clothing and shelter. Linen, cotton, rubber and lumber come from plants. Paper, perfume, paint, popcorn and medicines come from plants.

Thanks to plants we have tea, coffee, cocoa, fruit juices and many other things to drink.

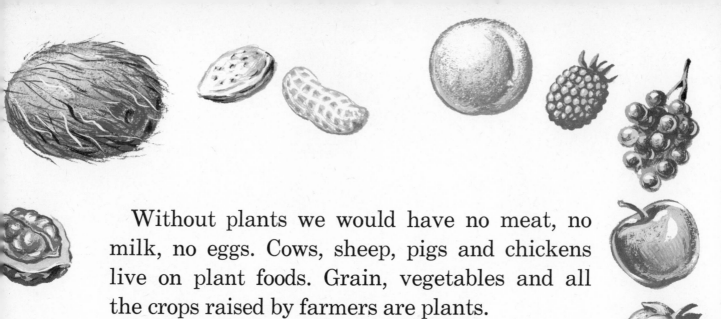

Without plants we would have no meat, no milk, no eggs. Cows, sheep, pigs and chickens live on plant foods. Grain, vegetables and all the crops raised by farmers are plants.

A cover of plant life keeps soil from blowing or washing away. Plant life holds water in the soil and helps to keep heavy rains from turning into floods.

The exciting world of the Plant Kingdom affects everyone every day.

No matter where we live each of us can find some growing thing. Even in the heart of a big city there are many plants to be found.

Examine the pattern of a leaf. Find the delicate pollen cases on a flower. Watch a fiddlehead unfurl. Or follow the flight of a seed sailing in the breeze. To do so is to enter the wonderland of plants.

FERNS

SEED BEARERS